# The Little Book of Lager

# THE LITTLE BOOK OF
# Lager

## ROD GREEN

EBURY PRESS

First published in the United Kingdom in 2001

Text © Rod Green, 2001

First published by Ebury Press
Random House, 20 Vauxhall Bridge Road,
London SW1V 2SA

Random House Australia (Pty) Limited
20 Alfred Street, Milsons Point, Sydney,
New South Wales 2061, Australia

Random House New Zealand Limited
18 Poland Road, Glenfield, Auckland 10, New Zealand

Random House South Africa (Pty) Limited
Endulini, 5a Jubilee Road, Parktown 2193, South Africa

Random House Group Limited Reg. No. 954009

13579108642

www.randomhouse.co.uk
A CIP catalogue record for this book is available from the British
Library.

ISBN 0 09 187955 8
Printed and bound in Denmark by Nørhaven A/S

To Morgan Academy Former Pupils Rugby Club where my drinking career started in earnest

# INTRODUCTION

'Would you like a beer or a lager?' how many times has some ignoramus (that's a plonker not a huge mouse) asked you that? It's incredible how many dyed-in-the-wool Brit bitter drinkers still look down on lager as being some sort of inferior foreign concoction.

Lager brewing has been going on for hundreds of years and, despite the fact that so many people here still regard it as a fizzy pale substitute for 'real beer', more lager is brewed around the world today than any other kind of beer. Brewers in a multitude of nations produce a huge diversity of wonderful lager beer.

'Bock', 'bak', 'hell', and 'dunkel' might sound like your drunken uncle falling down the stairs but they are actually all different lagers. A wide range of different tastes and textures cohabit beneath the lager umbrella – it isn't just the light-coloured sparkly stuff you drink to quench your thirst on a hot and sunny afternoon. Any overpaid smart-arse who just thought, 'No – that's champagne,' donate your next week's wages (or trust fund cheque) to charity and buy everyone in your local a pint tonight as punishment.

There are red lagers rosy as a boozer's nose, dark lagers black as Irish stout and lagers so strong that they'll melt your socks clean off.

Far from being a poor relation to ale, lager could be said to have saved the whole beer business. In times gone by, beer could only be brewed effectively during certain months as fermentation was so temperature sensitive. In the hot summer months fermentation could go badly wrong and the beer would be spoiled. Attempts were made to control the fermentation by carrying out the process in cool underground caves.

It was soon noticed that this cool fermentation made some types of yeast sink to the bottom of the beer instead of floating on the top as usual. Bottom fermentation (previously only known as a troubling disturbance in the trouser department) produced a different kind of beer that could be stored for longer without it going off – the word lager comes from the German word meaning a bed, resting place, or storage space. Indeed, because cold fermentation takes longer, the beer had to be stored and left to mature.

All that was in the 16th century and there have been numerous important refinements to the process since, but the lessons learnt through the discovery of lagering and cold storage were adapted to help stop other beers from going off in warm weather.

Nowadays, lager is brewed all over the world, including the UK. Although there are relatively few British lagers compared with the vast range of ales produced here, huge quantities of lager are brewed in this country including famous brands like Budweiser, Miller and Stella Artois as well as a plethora of supermarket own brands.

There are so many lagers produced, in fact, that it would be impossible to include them all in *The Little Book Of Lager*, otherwise it would have to be a bit bigger and renamed *The Utterly Humungously Huge Pick-me-up-for-a-hernia Book Of Lager* and by the time you'd read this far you'd be screaming for a truss.

So, if you come across a lager not listed in The World Of Lager A-Z, don't be surprised, just drink it!

# The World of Lager A-Z

80% of the world's surface is covered in water. The rest is lager . . .

# A is for . . .

| | |
|---|---|
| *Africana* | **Argentina** |
| *Adambraü* | **Austria** |
| *Adler* | **Belgium** |
| *Astika* | **Bulgaria** |
| *Alpine Lager* | **Canada** |
| *Ancla* | **Colombia** |
| *Alt Brummer Gold* | **Czech Republic & Slovakia** |
| | |
| *Asmara Lager* | **Eritrea** |
| *Ackerland, Adelscot,* | |
| *Ambre de Flandres, Ancre* | **France** |
| *Altstadthof Hausbier,* | |
| *Alt Wetzlar, Astra,* | |
| *Ayinger Altbayerische* | |
| *Dunkel* | **Germany** |

| | |
|---|---|
| *Aegean* | **Greece** |
| *Asahi* | **Japan** |
| *Allsopp's White Cap* | **Kenya** |
| *Aldaris* | **Latvia** |
| *Aass Bock, Arctic Pils,* | |
| *Alfa Edel Pils,* | **Norway** |
| *Amstel* | **Netherlands** |
| *Aguila, Amber, Alhambra* | **Spain** |
| *Amarit* | **Thailand** |
| *Amber Pilsner* | **Ukraine** |
| *Abita Golden Lager,* | |
| *Adirondack Amber,* | |
| *Amber,* | |
| *Anchor Steam Beer,* | |
| *Auburn Ale, Augsburger* | **United States** |

Beer has been around as long as civilisation and is referred to in Sumerian texts from around 6,000 years ago. This would have been a fairly basic ale. It has been suggested (in the pub the other night) that the ancient writings translated as

'This ale's crap. I could murder a lager.'

'Must have had a bad pint last night . . .' is the sorry cry of many a fuzzy-headed hangover sufferer on the morning after. You wouldn't have had that excuse in ancient Babylon. They took their beer seriously and brewing sub-standard booze was a serious criminal offence. Brewers could be sentenced to be drowned in their own beer.

Careful master brewers who survived, though, couldn't stop ale from going off in hot weather. They'd have to wait over 3,000 years for the invention of lager to help eradicate that problem.

Imagine waiting all that time for a pint only to discover that nobody had invented crisps yet . . .

Steam beer is so named not because it gets you steamin', although it certainly can, but because of the noise like hissing steam that could be heard in a bar when the casks were tapped. Steam beer is a Californian invention and is really a cross between a lager and an ale.

The first canned lager started to appear
in the 1930s, but they had to be opened
with a tin opener because the ringpull
had yet to be invented.

An excess of lager may inhibit sexual reproduction in humans, but lager wouldn't exist without its own form of reproduction. Yeast is what produces alcohol when hops, malt and water are fermented together. Yeast is a living organism and as it reproduces, it consumes the sugar in the malt. The yeast's waste products are alcohol and carbon dioxide.

# The World of Lager A-Z

Try them all before you die

## B is for . . .

| | |
|---|---|
| *Blue Label,* | |
| *Broken Hill Draught* | **Australia** |
| *Biekhart Cerveza Pilsen* | **Argentina** |
| *Bel Pils, Bokkereyer* | **Belgium** |
| *Belikin Beer* | **Belize** |
| *Burgasko Lager* | **Bulgaria** |
| *Brahma Pilsner* | **Brazil** |
| *Banks Lager Beer* | **Barbados** |
| *Brasal Bock,* | |
| *Brasal Légière, Brick Bock,* | |
| *Brick Premium Lager* | **Canada** |
| *Baiyun Beer* | **China** |
| *Bavaria Gold Beer* | **Costa Rica** |
| *Budweiser Budvar* | **Czech Republic** |
| *Black Regent* | **& Slovakia** |
| *Bjørne Bryg* | **Denmark** |
| *Bohemia Cerveza* | **Dominican** |
| | **Republic** |

| | |
|---|---|
| *Beck's, Bitburger, Brauhernen Pilsner, Braumeister, Brinkhoff's No1, Busch Golden Pilsner* | **Germany** |
| *Bak* | **Hungary** |
| *Birra Moretti, Bruna, Birra Peroni* | **Italy** |
| *Bintang* | **Indonesia** |
| *Baltijas* | **Latvia** |
| *Bofferding Lager Pils* | **Luxembourg** |
| *Birzicie* | **Lithuania** |
| *Blue Marlin* | **Mauritius** |
| *Bohemia* | **Mexico** |
| *Brand* | **Netherlands** |
| *Bargenbier* | **Romania** |
| *Bosun's* | **South Africa** |
| *Biere Benin* | **Togo** |
| *Baderbräu, Banquet Beer, Big Butt Doppel-bock, Bohemian Dunkel, Brooklyn Lager, Budweiser* | **United States** |
| *BGI* | **Vietnam** |
| *Bohlinger's* | **Zimbabwe** |

Prohibition, the Great Depression, mergers and closures meant that poor old Brooklyn lost all of its 40 breweries until the 1980s when Brooklyn Lager went into production and brought brewing back to the New York borough.

There are now around 1,000 breweries in the United States.
A century ago there were 4,000.

Pils, Pilsener, Pilsner and Pilsen
(all spelt much the same but sounding
slightly different) all take their name from
the town of Plzen
(spelt differently and sounding like a wet fart)
in the Czech Republic.

Holsten's Diät Pils caused some confusion when it was launched in the UK as lager drinkers anxious to shed a couple of pounds thought that it was a slimming aid. In fact, it's no good for that at all. Although most of the sugar is lost in fermentation, there are plenty of calories in the alcohol.

The lager was actually intended for diabetics, not slimmers. The Diät part of the name has now been dropped.

Danish brewer Jacob Christian Jacobsen welcomed his son into the family business by building him his own brewery. How grateful would you be to your dad for building you a brewery? Still, let's not start getting all jealous. The wee lad was only five. Jacob's son was called Carl and the brewery was built on a hill, or 'berg', which is why it ended up being called Carlsberg. It's really just as well his son wasn't called Dick and the brewery built on a headland.

Beers can sometimes be used instead of wine in cooking. The desert zabaglione is known as Beer Froth when dark lager is used to make it in Kaltenberg Castle's restaurant.

In America they love their lager so much they don't just drink it, they eat it, too. Beer soup made with cheese as well as the usual vegetable suspects features on a number of restaurant menus.

# The World of Lager A-Z

80% of the world's surface is covered in wate
The rest is lager . . .

# C is for . . .

| | |
|---|---|
| *Castelmaine XXXX* | **Australia** |
| *Cascade, Columbus* | **Austria** |
| *Corsendonk* | **Belgium** |
| *Canadian Lager,* | |
| *Carling Black Label* | **Canada** |
| *Cassovar, Crystal ,* | |
| *Cernohorsky Lezak* | **Czech Republic** |
| | **& Slovakia** |
| | |
| *Canton Lager Beer,* | |
| *Chinese Ginseng Beer,* | |
| *Chu Sing* | **China** |
| *Carlsberg, Ceres* | |
| *Royal Export* | **Denmark** |
| *Carling Black Label* | **England** |
| *Cuivrée* | **France** |

| | |
|---|---|
| CD, Carolus, Celebrator, Clausthaler, Cluss Bock | **Germany** |
| Crystal | **Italy** |
| Cobra | **India** |
| Chateau Neubourg, Christoffel | **Netherlands** |
| Cisk | **Malta** |
| Corona Extra, Cuzco | **Mexico** |
| Cergal, Cristal, Coral | **Portugal** |
| Corona | **Puerto Rico** |
| Cruzcampo | **Spain** |
| Camel Beer | **Sudan** |
| Castle Lager, Golden Pilsner Castle | **South Africa** |
| Cardinal | **Switzerland** |
| Castello | **Switzerland** |
| Carib | **Trinidad** |
| Club Pilsner | **Uganda** |
| Christian Moerlein, Cold Spring Export Lager, Coors, Celis Golden | **United States** |

The United States produces more beer
than any other nation with an annual
output of over 230 million hectolitres.
A hectolitre is 100 litres and there are
1.76 pints to a litre so that's 1.76 x 230
million x 100 = 40,480,000,000 pints.
A hell of a booze up!

You'll never stand at a bar enjoying a pint
with someone who suffers from potophobia –
it's a fear of drinks. Pocketphobia, on the
other hand, is just a fear of paying for drinks.
Avoid them, too.

Around half of the beer sold in the
United States is Budweiser.

While Brits might often consider lager to be something of a girlie drink with darker beers being a real man's drink, in the Czech Republic, home of the lager, their darker lager brews are widely considered to be ladies' drinks.

When out for a Chinese meal with a few
close friends, you might order the
Chinese beer Tsingtao. This very
drinkable lager comes from the port of
Qingdao (formerly known as Tsingtao)
where a brewery was set up by the
Germans, who invaded the area in the
19th century and later leased the port
from the Chinese in much the same
way that the British leased Hong Kong.
Your friends will be delighted to have
you tell them all about this, but probably
only if there has been a very long and
awkward lull in the conversation. Expect
another one as soon as you've finished.

# The World of Lager A-Z

Try them all before you die

# D is for . . .

| | |
|---|---|
| *Dogbolter* | **Australia** |
| *Double Happiness* | |
| *Guangzhou Beer* | **China** |
| *Dansk Dortmunder* | **Denmark** |
| *Démon* | **France** |
| *DAB, Delicator,* | |
| *Dom Pilsner* | **Germany** |
| *Dreher Pils* | **Hungary** |
| *Dvaro* | **Lithuania** |
| *Diekirch Exclusive* | **Luxembourg** |
| *Drei Hoefijzers* | **Netherlands** |
| *DB Export Dry* | **New Zealand** |
| *Dos Equis* | **Mexico** |
| *Dreikönigs, Dunkel Perle* | **Switzerland** |
| *Dortmunder Gold,* | |
| *Dundee's Honey* | |
| *Brown Lager* | **United States** |

The first lager ever produced was
brewed in Bavaria almost 500 years
ago by monks, possibly the
Holy Brothers of the Ringpull Tinnie.

Most of us are content just to drain the contents of a bottle of lager and, if we are ecologically sympathetic and politically right on, dump the bottle in the correct-colour glass recycling bin outside our local supermarket. There are those, however, who will carefully soak, steam or peel the treasured labels off the bottles in order to add them to their collections. One Norwegian collector has in excess of 320,000 beer labels.

In the 1958 World War II movie
*Ice Cold In Alex*, John Mills evades German
planes, dodges German patrols, tip-toes
through German minefields and puts up with
a German spy in his ambulance crew in order
to reach Alexandria and enjoy an ice-cold
German-style lager!
(It was actually Carlsberg)

Frustrated by the fact that its lagers were not available in Thailand due to import restrictions, the giant Heineken corporation solved the problem by building its own brewery there in 1995.

Kilarney's might sound as black and Irish as Guinness or Murphy's but it's actually a red lager produced in the US using Irish malts.

# The World of Lager A-Z

80% of the world's surface is covered in water. The rest is lager . . .

# E is for . . .

| | |
|---|---|
| *Eagle Blue Ice,* | |
| *Eagle Super, Emu, 1857* | **Australia** |
| *Edelweiss Bock* | **Austria** |
| *Emperor's Gold Beer* | **China** |
| *Elephant* | **Denmark** |
| *EKU Pils, Euler Landpils,* | |
| *Einbecker Maibock,* | |
| *Einbecker Urbock* | **Germany** |
| *Egils Pilsner* | **Iceland** |
| *Egelantier* | **Netherlands** |
| *Ekstra* | **Lithuania** |
| *EB Specjal Pils,* | |
| *Eurospecjal* | **Poland** |
| *Edel, Estrella Damm* | **Spain** |
| *Eichof Lager* | **Switzerland** |

| | |
|---|---|
| *Efes Pilsener* | **Turkey** |
| *ESB* | **Uganda** |
| *East Side Dark,* | |
| *Eliot Ness,* | |
| *Esquire Extra Dry* | **United States** |

Carlsberg's Elephant Beer is not named as a prediction of the massive hangover you can get by drinking more of this strong (7.5%) lager than is good for you. It's actually named after the life-sized stone(d?) elephants which stand either side of the main gate of Carlsberg's brewery in Copenhagen. The elephants appear to be pissed and playing football. Well why not? Isn't this the city that greets those arriving by sea with the sight of a woman who's actually half fish?

Most modern Japanese breweries
(Japan is the world's fourth largest
brewing nation) were built by the
Germans.

# LAGER COCKTAILS

## *Snakebite.....................*

Half a pint of lager mixed with half a
pint of cider

Verdict: An interesting combination of
the soft sweetness of the cider and the
edgy bitterness of the lager which
retains the bubbling effervescence
(provided a sparkling cider is used) of
both drinks. Well, you can say what
you like about the taste, this was
invented by kids who wanted to get
pissed quickly. Less popular nowadays
due to the widespread availability of
stronger lagers and alcopops.

Cracking open a few cans while you
watch the match with a couple of
mates? Raise a toast to
Ermal Cleon Fraze.
No, he didn't play for Ajax in the
1930s, he was much more
important than that . . .
in 1959 he invented the ringpull.

That first golden lager was produced by a Bavarian brewer, Joseph Groll, working in the Bohemian town of Plzen, which would later become part of the Czech Republic. At one time the colour might not have been too important because beer was drunk from tankards or mugs made from, for example, earthenware, ceramics or metal – things that were not transparent. In Bohemia, however, they also made glass and mass production of glass was leading to it becoming cheap enough for everyday use in drinking vessels. Once you could see the colour as well as judging the beer by smell and taste, golden lager really came into its own.

# The World of Lager A-Z

Try them all before you die

**F** is for . . .

| | |
|---|---|
| *Foster's* | **Australia** |
| *Five Star* | **China** |
| *Faxe Premium* | **Denmark** |
| *Freedom Pilsener* | **England** |
| *Fischer* | **France** |
| *Feldschlössen Pilsner,* | |
| *First, Franz Joseph* | |
| *Jubelbier, Freiberger Pils,* | |
| *Fürstenberg Pilsner* | **Germany** |
| *Flying Horse* | **India** |
| *Flag* | **Morocco** |
| *Flame* | **New Zealand** |
| *Frydenlund Pilsener* | **Norway** |
| *Forester's* | **South Africa** |
| *Falcon Export* | **Sweden** |

Lagers traditionally came in different colours depending in which region they were made. Munich lagers, for example, were dark brown, Vienna lagers were a reddish colour and those originating from Plzen, of course, were golden.

The Beer Barrel Saloon in Ohio, USA
has the world's longest bar at just
under 124 metres.
That's a long way to slide a lager.

Spoiling yourself again with an exotic Indian curry and washing it down with the equally exotic Indian Kingfisher lager? Fooling yourself more like. The most popular Indian meal is Chicken Tikka Masala, devised by Bangladeshi cooks in the UK especially for Brits and Kingfisher is now brewed in Kent by Shepherd Neame. Well, if it all tastes good, why not just get stuck in?

Upset that the Kingfisher you enjoy with your curry hasn't come all the way from India? You might decide to change to Cobra, the Indian lager which purports to be available in 90% of all top Indian restaurants. Like Kingfisher, it's a lovely lager for a curry but, also like Kingfisher, it's now brewed in this country and has been since 1997.

A lager's strength, like most other alcoholic drinks, is usually measured as a percentage of ABV – Alcohol By Volume.
4-5% is about average and anything of around 6% or more is fairly strong. Wine, of course, can easily be 12-13% or more, but needn't be twice as intoxicating because you don't drink wine by the pint . . . or do you?

# The World of Lager A-Z

80% of the world's surface is covered in water. The rest is lager . . .

## G is for . . .

| | |
|---|---|
| *Gold Fassl Pils, Gosser* | **Austria** |
| *Granville Island Dark Bock* | **Canada** |
| *Guangminpai* | **China** |
| *Gamle Special Dark* | **Denmark** |
| *Giraf, Grøn* | **Denmark** |
| *Goldenberg* | **France** |
| *Gilde Pils* | **Germany** |
| *Gulder* | **Ghana** |
| *Gocseji Barna* | **Hungary** |
| *Gull* | **Iceland** |
| *Gran Riserva* | **Italy** |
| *Gouverneur, Grolsch, Gulpener* | **Netherlands** |
| *Gdanskie* | **Poland** |
| *Growlin Gator Lager, Genny Bock* | **United States** |

The world's strongest lager is reputed
to be the Swiss brew Samichlaus.
At 14% ABV it is around three times as
strong as most other lagers.
Samichlaus means Santa Claus when
you're shit-faced.

# Lager Cocktails

## *Lager and Lime................*

1 Pint of lager and a dash of
lime cordial

Verdict: Can make a refreshing
precursor to a mad-as-a-Viking lager
session if you are hot and thirsty and
want to take some of the bite out of a
particularly gassy first pint. Don't waste
a decent lager this way.

Lager ahoy! In Darwin, Australia, a boat race is held for rafts made of beer cans and no doubt crewed by those who consumed the contents.

Ice beer is so named not because once you've had a few your legs start to act like you're standing on sheet ice, but because of the way it's made. A relatively new form of lager, it began to be introduced in the 1990s.

The lager is frozen during maturation and the ice crystals removed prior to bottling to make the beer stronger.

Tennent's produced an ice beer in 1996 with and ABV of 8.6% and called it Super Ice, also known as WHOOPS, as in 'I'll have another one of those . . . whoops!!'

The combined output of Britain's brewers easily puts us in the top five of the world's beer producing nations, although we struggle to make it into the top ten when it comes to average consumption.
Come on – drink for Britain!

# The World of Lager A-Z

Try them all before you die

# H is for . . .

| | |
|---|---|
| *Hahn* | **Australia** |
| *Hirter, Hopfenperle* | **Austria** |
| *Hua Nan Beer* | **China** |
| *Hof* | **Denmark** |
| *Hacker-Pschorr Hell,* | |
| *HB Hofbräuhaus München,* | |
| *Holsten Pils, Hubertus* | **Germany** |
| *Harp, Hoffman's Lager* | **Ireland** |
| *Hite* | **Korea** |
| *Henri Funck* | **Luxembourg** |
| *Hansa Urbock* | **Namibia** |
| *Heineken* | **Netherlands** |
| *Hansa Eksportol* | **Norway** |

| | |
|---|---|
| *Herbowe, Hevelius* | **Poland** |
| *Hopfenperle, Hubertus,* | |
| *Hürlimann* | **Switzerland** |
| *Helles Gold, Hell Lager* | **United States** |
| *Hunter's Lager* | **Zimbabwe** |

The world's most northerly lager is Lapin Kulta, brewed in Lapland.

The name Dos Equis, the Mexican lager brewed in an Austrian style (Mexico was once a colony of Austria), means two crosses and, sure enough, two big red crosses appear on the label. This does not mean it can be used in First Aid (thirst aid, maybe) but stems from an age-old European tradition of blessing beer by marking crosses on the barrels. The crosses also denoted the strength of the beer.

The term 'lager louts' may have given lager a downmarket association in the UK, but lager has a far loftier status in Germany. The Kaltenberg Castle brewery in Munich produces a number of different lagers and is run by Crown Prince Luitpold of the Bavarian royal family. Of course, there is no longer any Bavarian throne to which the Crown Prince could accede, but he's still pretty posh compared to your average Millwall supporter.

You'd be hard pressed to try to figure out
what the most commonly available
manufactured product in the country was.
Shoes? Clothes? Bread? In Kenya, it's beer.

That wedge of lime jammed into the neck of your bottle of lager isn't a new idea, although it has enjoyed something of a renaissance in recent years.
Some believe the lime is there to kill any bacteria around the mouth of the bottle, but the practice was actually a promotional ploy for a Mexican lager in the 1950s, reflecting the way that Tequila is served with salt and lime.

# The World of Lager A-Z

80% of the world's surface is covered in water. The rest is lager . . .

**I** is for . . .

| | |
|---|---|
| *Island Lager* | **Canada** |
| *Italia Pilsner* | **Italy** |
| *Imperator* | **Netherlands** |
| *Iron City Lager* | **United States** |

The world's most famous beer brewer, Anheuser-Busch, also owns a number of theme parks including Busch Gardens in Florida. The world's most famous beer drinker, Homer Simpson, guzzles Duff beer and in *The Simpsons* series 4, episode 13, 'Selma's Choice', Madge's sister Selma takes Bart and Lisa to a theme park called Duff Gardens.

There, our lawyers insist we point out, all similarities end.

In a recent survey, 80% of lager drinkers said they would rather drink bottled than tinned beer.

'Sorry, mate, it's got to be cash.'
How many times have you had a
plumber or a joiner or a builder hit you
with that immortal line just after the bank
has closed and you've only got enough
for that evening's grog guzzling down the
Dog & Strumpet? Well, next time just
bung him a couple of lagers.
The word cash is thought to come from
ancient Egypt where stonemasons were
paid with a kind of beer called Kash.

San Miguel, as countless millions of Spanish holidaymakers know it, is a pale golden lager best enjoyed while reading the *Daily Mirror* by the swimming pool, but San Miguel is also a dark beer (although still a lager) brewed in the Philippines.

Many years ago at the Pinkus Müller
brewery in Münster, the story goes that a
huge booze-up culminated with some
bloke who ran a zoo getting hold of a
donkey and painting stripes on it so that it
looked like a zebra.
He then tied a servant to its back.
Who said those Germans didn't have a
sense of humour?
The donkey, however, had seen it all
before and wasn't amused.
He said, 'He-haw, he-haw, he halways
does this when he's pissed!'

# The World of Lager A-Z

Try them all before you die

**J** is for . . .

| | |
|---|---|
| *James Boag's* | **Australia** |
| *Jupiler* | **Belgium** |
| *Jade* | **France** |
| *Jever* | **Germany** |
| *Jubilee* | **India** |
| *Jubileeuw* | **Netherlands** |
| *Jax* | **United States** |

# LAGER COCKTAILS

## *Lager tops...............*

An inch or so of lemonade in a pint glass which is then topped up with lager

Verdict: More beery than a full-on lager shandy and tempting for those with a sweet tooth but really only any use when the available lager isn't up to scratch. Can make a poor lager drinkable although usually just makes it worse. Used to be ordered by those who thought it could let them squeeze in another pint and still be under the limit for driving home, but they're all now in jail.

The 'Urquell' part of Pilsner Urquell is not the sound it makes as you pour it down your neck, but means 'original source' and identifies it as a Pilsner that actually does come from Plzen.

There are a multitude of different styles of beer drunk around the world but more lager is drunk than all of the other types of beer put together.

Depending on the strength and style of the beer, a pint of lager may have taken anything from a month to almost a year to pass through the brewery.
It can pass through you almost as quickly as it takes to say,
'Your round. Mine's a lager.
I'm off for a slash.'

The word 'Hell' on a German lager
doesn't mean that this is the drink of
the devil, it means that the lager is light
or clear as opposed to a
darker colour.

# The World of Lager A-Z

80% of the world's surface is covered in water. The rest is lager . . .

# K is for . . .

| | |
|---|---|
| *Keller Brau, Kaiser* | **Austria** |
| *Kalik Gold* | **Bahamas** |
| *Kaiser Gold* | **Brazil** |
| *Kamenitza Lager* | **Bulgaria** |
| *Keo* | **Cyprus** |
| *Kongens Bryg* | **Denmark** |
| *Koff, Karhu 3, Karjala* | **Finland** |
| *Kronenbourg* | **France** |
| *Kaiserdom, Kaiser Pilsner, Kaltenberg, König Ludwig Dunkel, König Pilsener, Kräusen, Kronen Classic, Kulminator 28* | **Germany** |
| *Kanizsai Korona* | **Hungary** |

| | |
|---|---|
| *Kronen* | **Italy** |
| *Kaliber* | **Ireland** |
| *Kingfisher* | **India** |
| *Kirin, Kuro-nama* | **Japan** |
| *Kaper, Krowleskie, Krakus* | **Poland** |
| *Kilsch Lager* | **United States** |

Germany and Czechoslovakia vie with each other for the title of 'The Most Beer Drunk Per Capita' with Germany now edging ahead with over 250 pints drunk per annum for every man, woman and child in the country. Germany should have profited in the drinking league when East and West were unified, but the East Germans drank less, dragging the German average down.

Czechoslovakia, on the other hand, did rather better when the Czechs formed their own republic and lost the Slovaks who spent more time on wine drinking than beer swilling. The Czech Republic's average, therefore, improved.

Not to be outdone, the Germans started drinking themselves into oblivion to clinch the title. Watch out for more European political manoeuvring, border shifting and all-out armed conflict as the beer battle continues . . .

The Czechs and the Germans may be
fiercely competitive about their beer
drinking reputations,
but their neighbours in Poland take
beer really seriously, even voting into
parliament several members of the
Beer Drinkers' Party.

Lager drinkers, of course, drink for the
pleasure of savouring a refreshing
golden brew, not to get smashed but
when you're enjoying a fine evening of
lager tasting and one pint turns
to three and three turn to six,
you just might end up having
'One over the eight' as the saying goes.
And why does the saying go like that?
It stems from an age-old belief that a
man should be able to handle eight pints
without too much trouble and anyone
seen in a falling-down drunken
mess had obviously had
'One over the eight'.

The most lager drinkers you will ever
find gathered in one place on a regular
basis will probably be in the world's
biggest pub, the Mathäuser in Munich.
It can seat 5,000 and serves over
84,000 pints a day.

The top five brewers in the world produce enough lager on an annual basis to float the proverbial battleship. In fact, they could float a whole fleet of battleships. They are:

1. Anheuser-Busch (USA)
2. Heineken (Netherlands)
3. Miller (USA)
4. Kirin (Japan)
5. Bond (Australia)

# The World of Lager A-Z

Try them all before you die

## L is for . . .

| | |
|---|---|
| *Loaded Dog Steam Beer,* | |
| *Longbrew* | **Australia** |
| *Labbatt's* | **Canada** |
| *La Bière Amoureuse* | **France** |
| *Leningrad Cowboy,* | |
| *Lapin Kulta* | **Finland** |
| *Lammsbräu Pils,* | |
| *Löwenbräu* | **Germany** |
| *Luxembourg* | **Luxembourg** |
| *Lente Bok* | **Netherlands** |
| *Leopard Black Label,* | |
| *Lion Ice* | **New Zealand** |
| *Lion Lager* | **Nigeria** |
| *Ludwig Pils, Lapin Kulta* | **Norway** |
| *Lech Pils, Lech Premium* | **Poland** |
| *Löwenbräu* | **Switzerland** |
| *Lone Star, Legacy Lager* | **United States** |

# Lager Cocktails

## *Stellabu* ..........................

1 pint Stella Artois
and a measure of (wait for it) Malibu

Verdict: This is the sort of thing that is
invented when mum and dad are at the
pictures and the kids raid the booze
cupboard. If you must try it,
keep a bucket handy.

Prominent Swiss brewer Hurlimann
(makers of the incredibly strong
Samichlaus) licensed Shepherd Neame in
Kent to brew lager bearing the
Hurlimann name.
It was renowned locally for its potency
and became known as
Hurlimann's Loony Juice.

The symbol which appears on the Japanese
Kirin lager is the Kirin, the half-dragon and
half-horse creature from which
the beer takes its name.
'Just trotting down to the pub, love . . .'

The Germans and the Dutch
have never been able to see eye to eye on
anything and that's especially true of beer.
While German bock beers are usually
lagers, Dutch bocks are normally top
fermenting ales and not lagers.
I suppose that was only to be expected.

Water is obviously a key ingredient in
lager and in Malta, where water isn't as
plentiful as they might like,
the Farson's brewery produces its Cisk
lager, along with its other beers, from
rainwater collected on the roof
and stored in huge underground
reservoirs.

# The World of Lager A-Z

80% of the world's surface is covered in water. The rest is lager . . .

# M is for . . .

| | |
|---|---|
| *Morchl* | **Austria** |
| *Maes Pils* | **Belgium** |
| *Molson,* | |
| *Moosehead Lager* | **Canada** |
| *Mon-Lei* | **China** |
| *Meteor, Mutzig, Mortimer* | **France** |
| *Maisel Pilsner,* | |
| *Meister Pils* | **Germany** |
| *McFarland* | **Italy** |
| *Mamba Lager* | **Ivory Coast** |
| *Mansfeld* | **Luxembourg** |
| *Maltezer* | **Netherlands** |
| *Mainland Dark* | **New Zealand** |
| *Mack Polar Bear* | **Norway** |
| *Magnat* | **Poland** |

| | |
|---|---|
| *Melo Abreu* | **Portugal** |
| *Moskovskoye* | **Russia** |
| *McEwan's Lager* | **Scotland** |
| *Mahou, Marlen* | **Spain** |
| *Matt's, Michelob, Miller,* | |
| *Meister Bräu* | **United States** |

The next time you pop the
overcomplicated swing top gimmick off
a Grolsch, insist on telling your friends
the terribly interesting fact that,
although it says Grolsch on the bottle,
the brewer is actually Grolsche.
They named themselves after the town
where they are based, Groenlo,
which doesn't sound that much like
Grolsche but the town was once called
Grolle, which is a bit closer.
Then, drink your friends' beer before
they wake up.

Different styles of German lager take their name from the towns where they were developed, just as the Hamburger and Frankfurter have done in the burger and sausage business. We therefore have bottles bearing the names Dortmunder from Dortmund, Freiberger from Freiberg and Ayinger from Aying. It's really just as well that no beer of note ever came from the famous old German town of Wank.

Budweiser is produced by Anheuser-Busch (biggest brewer in the world) but Budweiser Budvar comes from the town of Budweis in the Czech Republic. They have had a running battle for years over who should own the brand name Budweiser with the Czechs claiming that they should be allowed to use the name as Budweiser simply means 'from Budwar' as in Hamburger, Frankfurter, Dortmunder, etc., etc. The Americans, however, have been making Budweiser since about 1870, some 25 years before the Budvar brewery was founded. They, therefore, claim that the name is theirs and have tried to stop the Czechs from using it.

The plucky little Czechs, however, countered with the fact that the Samson brewery in Budweiser produced a beer which they marketed as Budweiser before the Americans, although Samson stopped using the name in the early 1900s. So, amid a great rattling of writs and with their lawyers laughing all the way to the bank, Annheuser-Busch have succeeded in stopping Budvar from marketing their beer in America and Budvar have registered the name for themselves everywhere they can find that the Americans haven't already got to. Budvar appears in America as 'Crystal' and Budweiser appears in countries such as Spain under the name 'Bud'.

The Swiss and the Germans both have
completely separate brewers and brews
called Löwenbräu, but they don't seem
to mind much.

The Eurocrats have ways of
quantifying everything to fit in with
regulations but you have to admire the
European Brewing Convention for
coming up with the grading system for
beer. It must have taken soooooooooo
much research . . . hic!
There are specific measurements for
colour and taste. Lager should have
5 to 10 units of colour and there are
over 120 recognised descriptions
for tasting beer.
Nice work if you can get it.

Although beer was first made in Africa (from malted barley cakes) it was the Europeans who took beer back there in a big way when they colonised so much of the continent. Breweries were set up all over Africa producing traditional lagers and the malted barley cakes were slowly forgotten about.

The term 'lager lout' was first used by
Tory MP John Patten.

# The World of Lager A-Z

Try them all before you die

# N is for . . .

| | |
|---|---|
| *Nine Star* | **China** |
| *Noordheim* | **France** |
| *Nastro Azzurro* | **Italy** |
| *Nugget Golden Lager* | **New Zealand** |
| *Ngoma* | **Togo** |
| *Nile Special* | **Uganda** |
| *Northwoods Lager* | **United States** |

Taking back the empties is a practice long forgotten in the UK as we tend to use bottle banks or buy our beer in cans, also now recyclable, but in Denmark they object to using cans as it is not deemed environmentally sound and beer is still bought in bottles that can be returned.

When pouring lager into a glass,
the glass should be slightly tilted and
the beer poured down the side of the
glass. This helps to release some of
the gas from the beer so that you don't
gulp it down and end up with a
stomach like a bouncy castle.
Straighten the glass towards the
end of pouring to give
the beer a nice head.

If you don't pour your lager correctly, or if you drink it straight from a can or a bottle, you may well end up bagged out with gas. This has two effects. Firstly, it fills you up, leaving less space in your stomach for more beer. Secondly, the gas will find a way out of your stomach (hopefully upwards towards your mouth, but downwards is always another option) and make you belch, although you are unlikely to equal the achievement of Mr Paul Hunn, the loudest burper in the world at 118.1 decibels.

The ideal temperature at which to serve lager is 5.5°C – that's the temperature of the lager, of course, not wherever you're serving it, so don't start looking at the weather forecast or switching off your heating . . .

Heineken is the world's largest brewer
outside of the United States.
The company has over 100 breweries
around the world and its beers are
available in 170 countries,
selling ten times as much abroad as
they do at home.

# The World of Lager A-Z

80% of the world's surface is covered in water. The rest is lager . . .

# O is for . . .

| | |
|---|---|
| *Original Chilli Beer* | **Australia** |
| *Ottakringer Helles* | **Austria** |
| *Okanagan Spring Pilsner* | **Canada** |
| *Optimator* | **Germany** |
| *Oranjeboom Pilsner* | **Netherlands** |
| *OK Jasne Pelne* | **Poland** |
| *Onix* | **Portugal** |
| *Ohlsson's Lager* | **South Africa** |
| *Old Milwaukee,* | |
| *Oktoberfest* | **United States** |

Lager brewer Prince Luitpold of
Bavaria holds a medieval jousting
tournament at his Kaltenberg Castle
each July where trained stuntmen
knock the stuffing out of each other in
front of 10,000 spectators.

More royal connections. Lager brewer Brand, now part of the giant Heineken corporation, is the official supplier of lager to the Dutch Monarchy.

Bock beers were originally strong lagers brewed by monks as their staple 'bread' to see them through the rigours of the lent fast. Drink enough of the stuff and you wouldn't care whether you hadn't eaten for a week, two weeks or two months.

In order to ensure the quality and purity of beer being produced, Count William IV of Bavaria introduced a law in 1516 determining exactly what ingredients could be used to produce beer. The law was to stand for over 450 years until it was overruled by the European Union. Despite the EEC ruling, many German brewers, and breweries around the world established by the Germans, adhere to the traditions established in the 16th century.

The famous Australian Foster's lager
was first produced down under by the
Foster brothers –
from New York, USA.

# The World of Lager A-Z

Try them all before you die

# P is for . . .

| | |
|---|---|
| *Power's* | **Australia** |
| *Privat Pils* | **Austria** |
| *Primus Pils* | **Belgium** |
| *Pacific Real Draft* | **Canada** |
| *Peking Beer* | **China** |
| *Pilsner Urquell* | **Czech Republic & Slovakia** |
| *Palmse* | **Estonia** |
| *Pilsner Nikolai* | **Finland** |
| *Pilsissimus,* | |
| *Pinkus Miller Spezial* | **Germany** |
| *Patriator, Pelforth Blonde,* | |
| *Pelican* | **France** |
| *Pilsener Mack-Ol* | **Norway** |
| *Peru Gold* | **Peru** |

| | |
|---|---|
| *Pripps Bla* | **Sweden** |
| *Pony* | **Switzerland** |
| *Premium Verum,* | |
| *Point Special,* | |
| *Pennsylvania Pilsner,* | |
| *Pearl Lager* | **United States** |
| *Polar Lager* | **Venezuela** |

Author Anthony Burgess named his novel *Time For A Tiger* after the slogan on the clock on the Singapore brewery where Tiger Beer is made.

# LAGER COCKTAILS

## *Light and Lager*.................

Half a pint of lager mixed with half a
pint of light ale

Verdict: A perky lager will certainly add
a little life to a listless light ale but the
mixture will usually result in a bland
and sterile hybrid which we can be
thankful will never breed.

Next time someone raises a glass in the bar and says, 'Here's to the boss because he's such a nice, generous bloke,' (no, you're right, now I think about it, I've never heard that either) or proposes some other toast and someone asks, 'Why is it called a toast?' you can tell them. It comes from a peculiar practice years ago whereby a savoury treat of spiced toast was dropped into your drink to add flavour and as a bit of a snack. Cheers on toast!

Tegestology may sound like a worrying
problem in your Y-fronts but it's
actually a lot more disturbing than that.
It's the study and collection
of beer mats.
One Austrian master tegestologist has
over 150,000 beer mats. That lot would
come in handy when you've got a few
mates round . . .

To go with your collection of beer mats, of course, you need a crisp packet collection. Frank Ritter from Nottingham has almost 700 different packets from 15 different countries.

Breweriana is a term familiar to tegestologists. It refers to all of the paraphernalia produced by a brewery from beer mats and matchbooks to t-shirts and parasols.
Collectors correspond the world over buying, selling and swapping breweriana. They really ought to get out down the pub more.

# The World of Lager A-Z

Try them all before you die

# R is for . . .

| | |
|---|---|
| *Red Ant, Reschs Pilsner* | **Australia** |
| *Reininghaus* | **Austria** |
| *Red Baron* | **Canada** |
| *Rebellion Lager, Red Erik* | **Denmark** |
| *Ruutli Olu, Reval* | **Estonia** |
| *Radeberger Pilsner,* | |
| *Ratskeller Edel-Pils,* | |
| *Ratsherrn,* | |
| *Reichelbräu Eisbock,* | |
| *Romer Pilsner, Rauchbier* | **Germany** |
| *Red Stripe* | **Jamaica** |
| *Raffo* | **Italy** |
| *Rheineck Lager* | **New Zealand** |
| *Ringnes Pils* | **Norway** |
| *Rex* | **Nigeria** |
| *Red Horse* | **Philippines** |
| *Rheingold* | **Switzerland** |
| *Rolling Rock,* | |
| *Royal Brand Beer* | **United States** |

Having had a few lagers the night before and feeling like some half human, half pond sludge thing that somehow slipped through the quality control check on God's production line, what you need is a 'hair of the dog'. It's not an attractive expression, is it? 'Petal of the daisy' or 'Alka of the seltzer' would sound far more appealing. 'Hair of the dog', however, is an ancient remedy, albeit for rabies, not a hangover. When bitten by a rabid dog, people believed that rubbing the bite with the burnt 'hair of the dog that bit you' would prevent you from catching the disease.

Bock beers, although historically not always lagers, take their name from Einbeck in northern Germany. When the style of beer was adopted by the Bavarians in the south, the pronunciation in their dialect turned 'beck' into 'bock'. A local footie team would no doubt have David Bockham playing at right bock.

Not only did the Bavarians change beck to bock because it was easier to say, but it meant that they could put a billy goat, also called a bock, on the labels of their beer. What appears to be a goat or ram's head still appears on many German bottle labels and logos.

Some bock beers have rather strange
names such as Kulminator, Triumphator,
Terminator or even Procrastinator.
The 'ator' suffix stems from a bock first
brewed by German monks who called it
Salvator, meaning saviour.

Bock beers are renowned for their
potency but don't expect a doppelbock
(doppel means double in German) to
be twice the strength of a normal bock.
It will be stronger, but not
twice as strong.

# The World of Lager A-Z

80% of the world's surface is covered in water. The rest is lager . . .

## S is for . . .

| | |
|---|---|
| *Southwark Premium* | **Australia** |
| *Swan Draught,* | |
| *Schlank & Rank, Sigl,* | |
| *Steffl, Stiegl Goldbräu* | **Austria** |
| *Signature Amber Lager* | **Canada** |
| *Sweet China, Sun Lik,* | |
| *Song Hay Double Happiness,* | |
| *Shanghai* | **China** |
| *Silver Pilsner* | **Denmark** |
| *Saku* | **Estonia** |
| *Sandels* | **Finland** |
| *Saaz, Septante Cinq* | **France** |
| *St George Keller Bier,* | |
| *St Jakobus, Salvator,* | |
| *Schultheiss Pilsner,* | |
| *Stauder Tag, Stephansquell* | **Germany** |

| | |
|---|---|
| *Siraly* | **Hungary** |
| *Sans Souci, Splügen* | **Italy** |
| *Sapporo , Shokusai* | |
| *Bakusha, Spring Valley,* | |
| *Suntory Daichi, Super Dry* | **Japan** |
| *Sirvenos* | **Lithuania** |
| *Sol, Superior* | **Mexico** |
| *Super Dortmunder* | **Netherlands** |
| *Steinlager* | **New Zealand** |
| *Star* | **Nigeria** |
| *Super Bock, Sagres* | **Portugal** |
| *San Miguel* | **Philippines** |
| *Schiehallion Lager* | **Scotland** |
| *San Miguel* | **Spain** |
| *Spendrup's* | **Sweden** |
| *Spiess Edelhell, Samichlaus* | **Switzerland** |
| *Singha* | **Thailand** |
| *Stroh's, Stoney's Lager,* | |
| *Stegmaier, Shiner Bock,* | |
| *Scrimshaw Pilsner, Schlitz,* | |
| *Schaefer Beer, Samuel* | |
| *Adams Boston Lager* | **United States** |
| *Simba* | **Zaire** |

# LAGER COCKTAILS

## *Lager and black...............*

1 pint of lager and a dash of
blackcurrant cordial

Verdict: A sickly sweet concoction
beloved of students and, therefore,
probably the forerunner of today's
alcopops. Turns your tongue and lips
black after a couple and if anybody
sees you throwing up in the street after
closing time, they think you have
massive internal bleeding because it
looks like you just deposited every drop
of blood in your body onto the
pavement.

If you're standing in a bar in Norway and you hear people yelling Aass Fatøl, don't get upset. It's not some strange Scandinavian insult, it is the most popular lager in Norway.

The word 'dunkel' appears on the labels of some German lager bottles and is the sound your head makes when it hits the floor after you've slightly misjudged your intake capacity. Coincidentally, it also means 'dark' in German and the lager in the bottle may well look more like stout.

If you are one of those blokes who thinks that girls drinking pints of lager is unladylike and ought not to be allowed, then think again. Lager can act as a kind of aphrodisiac. I don't mean that after you've had a few any bumfaced old hogwart starts to look attractive (lager can have this effect on both sexes), but lager contains hops and hops are one of the few foodstuffs which contain natural oestrogens.

Some believe that this oestrogen intake may boost a woman's feeling of femininity, making her feel good about herself and ultimately horny.

So for goodness sake let them drink lager if they want to!

If a lady friend does drink lager and
perhaps has one more than she may have
intended, rather than referring to her as
'lagered up', 'guttered', 'off her face'
or plain old 'pissed', it's more polite to say
that a lady is a little tiddly. This comes
from the rhyming slang for drink –
'tiddly wink'.

# The World of Lager A-Z

Try them all before you die

T is for . . .

| | |
|---|---|
| *Toohey's* | **Australia** |
| *Trumer Pils* | **Austria** |
| *Trapper Lager, True Bock* | **Canada** |
| *Tsingtao Beer, Tientan Beer* | **China** |
| *Tuborg* | **Denmark** |
| *Tume, Tartu Olu* | **Estonia** |
| *Tourtel, '33'* | **France** |
| *Triumphator* | **Germany** |
| *Talleros* | **Hungary** |
| *Tusker* | **Kenya** |
| *Tafel Lager* | **Namibia** |
| *Tecate* | **Mexico** |
| *Topazio* | **Portugal** |
| *Tennent's Lager* | **Scotland** |
| *Tiger* | **Singapore** |
| *Triple Bock, Tabernash* | **United States** |

Holding a glass of lager up to the light and admiring its sparkling golden colour is an essential part of the enjoyment of a pint. You should make sure, then, that your glass is clean. The whole ritual falls pretty flat if your dirty, smeared glass makes your lager look like the water the goldfish died in last week.

To keep your glass in tip-top sparkling condition, wash it in hot soapy water (or some prefer water with salt in it) and then rinse it thoroughly with cold water. Make sure you get all that detergent (or salt) off the glass as an accumulation of the stuff can build up after a few washes. Then allow the glass to drip dry on the draining board and don't be tempted to undo all your good cleaning work by smearing it with a manky old tea towel. If you live in an area where the water drying on the glass might leave a coating, try wiping the glass dry with a square of kitchen roll.

Good King Wenceslas (yes, the one
who looked out on the Feast of Stephen
in the Christmas carol) wasn't just a
good king to yonder peasant gathering
winter fuel out in the deep and crisp
and even snow – he was also a good
king for lager drinkers.
One of his descendants first granted
the right to brew beer to Plzen as it lay
in the Kingdom of Wenceslas.
One more time now
'Brightly shone the moon that night . . .'

Famous brewers of the golden throat
lubricant Heineken have their fingers in
rather a lot of pints including Irish stout
and ale brewers Murphy's. Heineken
acquired Murphy's in 1983.

French lagers traditionally come from
the Alsace region,
the area of France most influenced by
their German neighbours.
Kronenbourg and Fischer both have
breweries in the Strasbourg area.

There aren't too many British lagers that can claim a foothold on the world stage but surely Carling Black Label, footie sponsors and namesakes of England's bum-faced former rugby captain, is one of them.

Surely not. Carling is brewed in the UK but originally came from Canada.

# The World of Lager A-Z

Try them all before you die

# U & V are for . . .

| | |
|---|---|
| *Urbock 23* | **Austria** |
| *Vaakuma* | **Finland** |
| *Upstaal* | **France** |
| *Ureich Pils, Ur-Krostitzer,* | |
| *Urstoff* | **Germany** |
| *Viking Bjór* | **Iceland** |
| *Urtyp Pilsner* | **Netherlands** |
| *Voll-Damm* | **Spain** |
| *Vollmund* | **Switzerland** |

Statistics show that the Czechs and the Germans consume far more lager than the Brits, but other studies indicate that we tend to be more sociable about it, generally drinking more in pubs and bars than the Czechs and Germans.

That's why we have a long tradition of very funny comedians who have learnt their art standing at a bar, and why your average German comedian would struggle to raise a smirk in a snigger factory.

Plzen has a lot to boast about with the
hugely popular style of lager that has
been adopted by brewers all over the
world, but for a long time they kept quiet
about the other side of their industrial
heritage. The town is also home to the
Skoda factory.

Holiday lager Amstel, available in 75 different countries, is a fine, refreshing pint when you're running the sort of blood-boiling temperature that inadvertently witnessing topless sunbathers can induce, but beware if you decide to track down an Amstel in its home town of Amsterdam.

There you can find nine different types of Amstel – some of them not even lagers!

Despite the fact that your average German drinks enough lager every week to sink a U-boat and the country as a whole is one of the world's top beer brewing nations, none of the German brewers makes it into the world's top ten in production or sales terms as every German brewer faces competition in his home market from no less than 1200 rivals.

As well as Budweiser and Michelob, Anheuser-Busch produces around 30 different brews for the US market in 14 different breweries. Their original Brewery in St Louis is open to tourists and is home to the company's prized Clydesdale horses. Location of the company's famous Budweiser frogs is a closely guarded secret as the weasel is apparently still out to get them.

# The World of Lager A-Z

80% of the world's surface is covered in water. The rest is lager . . .

# W & X are for . . .

| | |
|---|---|
| *West End Draught* | **Australia** |
| *Weiselburger, Weihnachtsbock* | **Austria** |
| *West Lake Beer* | **China** |
| *Wel Scotch, Willfort* | **France** |
| *Warsteiner, Witzgall Vollbier* | **Germany** |
| *Werner Brau, Wuhrer Pilsner* | **Italy** |
| *Windhoek* | **Namibia** |
| *Xibeca* | **Spain** |
| *Wartek Lager* | **Switzerland** |
| *Wrexham Lager* | **Wales** |

# Lager Cocktails

## *Lager Float...........................*

1 pint lager with a scoop of ice cream
floating on top

Verdict: Yes, I know it sounds disgusting
but don't knock it till you've tried it.
Okay it *is* disgusting but we all have our
little foibles, don't we? It's got to be vanilla
ice cream, of course. That goes without
saying. Anything else would be horribly
revoltingly disgusting . . .

The poor man's black velvet
(Guinness and champagne) is how most
people used to regard a 'black and tan'
(Guinness and cider) but Michelob have a
different idea of what it should be.
The Black and Tan marketed by Michelob in
the US is a dark ale mixed with lager.

The giant Heineken corporation produces over 90 million hectolitres (hecto = 100) of beer per year. If you conscientiously drank 10 pints every night, you could polish off that lot on your own in just under four-and-a-half million years.

Describing downing a few lagers with your mates as 'going on a bender' doesn't actually refer to the bent and wobbly state you end up in, but to the regular bending of the elbow that is so necessary to get the aforementioned lager down your neck.

Although lager is more stable than
most types of beer once bottled,
it should not be allowed to sit in direct
sunlight, as strong light can cause a
reaction that will make the
beer go bad.

# The World of Lager A-Z

Try them all before you die

# Y & Z are for . . .

| | |
|---|---|
| *Zipfer* | **Austria** |
| *Zagorka Lager* | **Bulgaria** |
| *Yebisu* | **Japan** |
| *Zywiec Full Light* | **Poland** |
| *Zhigulevskoe* | **Russia** |
| *Zaragozana Export* | **Spain** |
| *Zambesi* | **Zimbabwe** |

Malt Liquor is a kind of lager brewed in America which is usually rather sweet and sugary and lacks the refreshing taste you'd expect of a normal beer. They are also usually pretty alcoholic and are renowned for providing a fast track to babbling incoherent drunkenness. Every cloud has a silver lining . . .

Rauchbier, or smoked beer, is not specifically produced to be drunk while puffing away on a Marlboro Light. The malt is cured over a beechwood fire to give the final brew a smoky taste.

Beer was introduced into Japan in 1853 by the American navy when they paid a friendly formal visit to the country. A delegation was invited on board and offered beer. They rather liked it. In 1869 an American company established a brewery in Yokohama which would later become Kirin.

# Lager Cocktails

## *Depth Charge*...........................

1 pint lager with a bit drunk out of the top
and a shot glass of vodka dropped in

Verdict: Generally drunk as a dare or in
a bar room drinking competition with a
maniac who hasn't been taking his
medication. Anyone who drinks one too
many Depth Charges (and one may well
be too many) will leave the pub, start
believing that he's being followed by
submarines that want revenge, and have
to zig-zag furiously to avoid being
torpedoed. The submarines then surface
looking for all the world like
traffic on the road.

Bohemia, birthplace of modern lager, is thought to have been brewing beer for almost 1200 years.

Starapromen is a Czech lager which is enjoying widespread popularity nowadays mainly due to the fact that Bass has invested heavily in the Czech brewery and is marketing the brand heavily internationally.

America's second biggest brewer,
Miller, is less than half the size of
Anheuser-Busch. Even so, Miller is still
the third largest brewer in the world.

If lager is the pint for you and you want to find out more about it, then get on the net. The major brewers all have fantastic websites and the minor brewers' sites are often even better.

You should also take a look at the following books which proved in valuable when researching *The Little Book of Lager*.

*Michael Jackson's Beer Companion*
by Michael Jackson,
published by Mitchell Beazley
*The Complete Guide to Beer*
by Brian Glover,
published by Lorenz Books
*Classic Bottled Beers of the World*
by Roger Potz,
published by Prion

## About the Author

Rod Green is a retired astronaut who applied to join NASA's Mars space programme after a bloke down the pub told him that the polar ice caps there were actually frozen lager. He left NASA on discoverng that being sealed into a spacesuit is the last thing you want the morning after a mighty vindaloo.

He lives in Surrey with his wife and son and a mounting overdraft.